Joanne Comeau

SO-EKN-809

Word Identification for Teachers

Marvin E. Oliver

Eastern Washington University

High Impact Press
Cheney, WA 99004

Published by
High Impact Press
Cheney, Washington 99004
Copyright © 1987 by High Impact Press.

All rights reserved. No part of this book may be reproduced in any form, electronic or mechanical, including photocopy, recording, or any information storage and retrieval system, without permission in writing from the publisher.

Library of Congress Catalog Card Number: 86-82262

International Standard Book Number: 0-935435-00-x

Printed in the United States of America

Preface

This little book contains some of the basic information that teachers need to know about word identification. It is more about what teachers need to know than about how to teach it. This book is intended for prospective teachers, classroom teachers, and reading specialists. It should be a valuable supplement to major textbooks on reading instruction. The information contained here is based on the following assumptions:

1. Reading is a meaningful response to words that is appropriate to the author's intended meaning. Reading is more than a process of arriving at the spoken counterpart of printed words.

2. Reading involves the processing of both visual and non-visual information. Non-visual information is what is in the reader's head: 1) knowledge of the world, and 2) linguistic awareness of English grammar. Visual information is obtained from the print on the page. The more non-visual information one has, the less visual information one needs, and visaversa. The beginning reader needs more information from the printed words than does the more experienced reader.

3. A knowledge of letter-sound relationships is essential to independence and power in reading. English is encoded with letters of the Roman alphabet. Letters and combinations of letters represent speech sounds. The main value of knowing letter-sound relationships, or phonics, is not to "sound-out" words but to understand why words are spelled the way they are. *Important for communication!*

4. The beginning reader must learn to hear the important sounds within spoken words in order for spelling to make sense or for phonics to be useful in learning to identify words.

5. Words stimulate thought and elicit images. Conflicts between meaning and letter-sound regularity in spelling favor meaning. *(Spelling based more upon meaning than the phonetics)*

Phonics useless for children would do not hear/perceive phonemes.

6. Word identification information for the teacher is based more
   on pedagogy (instructional practices) than it is on science.
   Linguists are scientists who study language. Teachers are
   more interested in helping children learn to read than they
   are in studying language. There are some differences between
   linguistic terminology and the terminology of reading teachers.

7. Teachers need to make a clear distinction between print and
   speech. Linguists generally agree that letters don't really
   talk. Letters neither make nor have sounds. Letters are used
   to represent speech sounds and meaning in words. Speech is
   primary.

8. Sounding out words is not reading. Teachers need to help
   lead children to an understanding of reading as a meaningful
   process.

9. All word identification activities should be conducted with
   positive affective objectives. Children do not learn to read
   by avoiding it. Help children to develop approach behaviors
   toward reading.

10. Word identification is only a means to a greater end:
    that of reading. As children increase their reading skill
    they have a declining need for phonics. In a sense, we are
    teaching children to avoid reliance upon phonics as they
    improve their reading skill.

CONTENTS

CHAPTER I

INTRODUCTION

Some beginning students of reading instruction seem understandably confused with the apparent paradox which implies that phonic knowledge is critical for the classroom teacher yet warns against excessive early emphasis on phonic knowledge in teaching children to read. Phonics is only one of several strategies used to mediate the identification of words.

Clarity lies somewhere in the understanding of the difference between means and ends, parts and wholes, and reading pedagogy (instruction) and functional reading. Phonic knowledge is a means to intermediate word identification or word analysis, which is a means to immediate word identification, which is a means to meaning identification, which, in turn, facilitates the accomplishment of the reading act as a means for getting information and enriching life.

The competent teacher of reading must have a thorough command of letter-sound relationships, the structure of words, and methods and strategies for teaching word analysis. This knowledge is expected to serve as a base, or thesaurus; a storehouse of information. The teacher can use this base as a source of reference for helping pupils to build the power of independence in word identification.

There is a difference between the phonic knowledge needed by the teacher, and that needed by the pupil who is developing functional word identification strategies. The competent teacher may be required to identify the digraphs in the word diphthong or to explain why the "ch" in school is not traditionally classified as a digraph by reading teachers. Yet, the pupil who can identify the word school upon sight may not become a better reader by being able to explain why the letters "ch" are not classified as a digraph by the teacher.

Children need to learn to analyze words for structure and for letter-sound relationships in order to develop independence in reading. The child who does not learn to analyze words and synthesize speech sounds into words (auditory blending or "sounding out") will be handicapped in ability to read independently. The danger in an overemphasis on phonics in reading instruction is that the child may come to perceive reading as "sounding out words" rather than a process of getting information or enjoying a story. Phonics is but one aspect of word analysis and word analysis is but one aspect of the reading program. The child who develops an excessive reliance upon phonic strategies for word identification may also be handicapped in ability to read independently.

It is recommended that the child's introduction to word identification be done with the learning of a few whole words. These words can later be used as a reference when learning word analysis techniques. Breaking words into parts is a higher level skill than is learning whole words. The learning of whole words provides the beginner with an immediate feeling of success because the child can say, "I know how to read some words," instead of, "I can say some speech sounds," or, "I learned some phonics."

Functional phonic knowledge is essential for development of the maximum word identification power. But such power does not necessarily emerge from drill on auditory blending or by learning to grunt, groan, spit, sputter, and cough in response to letters. Word identification techniques are most useful in reading when they are functional; that is, when the pupil has developed the strategies of separating distinctive features of words into significant and non-significant categories. Each individual learner must develop a personal list of those features which make a word appear unique. FISH, fish, Fish, fish, and *fish* are all members of the same set and all represent the same spoken word, no matter how large or small the size of the print or whether they are written with chalk or ink. In developing a concept of the printed word fish, the beginner must learn to overlook those features that are not significant. Much of this word-concept classification comes from practice in responding to and classifying features of words in meaningful context, i.e. reading.

The process of reading for meaning is much more than the sum of its parts because only the reader can decide which parts are essential to provide new information. Much of what the reader needs for the improvement of word identification is learned from feedback that can't be provided by an external source such as the teacher. But the competent teacher of reading will provide the opportunity for valuable practice and will know enough about phonics to be able to give the learner information when it seems appropriate.

Reading is much more than phonics but phonics is essential for reading. Social and personal adjustment require more than the use of reading, but reading is essential in order to function in our culture. Teachers are urged to learn all they can about phonics, word analysis strategies, and basic concepts of reading instruction in order to add to the qualities that are valued in the competent elementary teacher of reading.

Is Reading Really More than Word Identification?

Where does word identification fit into the reading process? Much of the strategy for teaching word identification will be influenced by the teacher's definition of reading. There is no universally acceptable definition of reading. We can "read a person like a book" by interpreting their posture and demeanor. We can read the expression on someone's face. There are people who can read tea leaves, palms of hands, shapes in clouds, and messages over Citizen's Band (CB) radio. But what teachers and parents usually think of as reading in school has to do with books and printer's ink. For the sake of measurement and comparison, reading is usually defined as scores on a reading survey test. The ability to read, however, involves more than answering test questions.

Elkonin's (1973) definition of reading, from a report on reading in the Soviet Union is, "Reading is the creation of the sound form of the word according to its graphic model" (p. 33). Soffietti (1958) stated that, "The linguist believes that the printed word acts as a trigger that releases its oral counterpart, which, in turn, releases a meaning that we already possess" (p.34). Charles Fries, the linguist upon whose ideas the Merrill Linguistic Reading Program is based, has described reading apart from the uses to which reading can be put. According to the late Charles Fries (1963), "The process of learning to read in one's own native language is the process of transfer from auditory signs for language signals, which the child has already learned, to new visual signs for the same signals" (p. 120). Fries probably did not mean, however, that word calling without a meaningful response is reading. It is likely he meant that the child who is reading is making the same meaningful response to the author's printed surface structure that could be made via the spoken equivalent.

Surface structure is a term that linguists use to refer to the arrangement of words. Printed surface structure is what you see as opposed to the meaning that it represents. Put another way, Fries explained, "One can 'read' insofar as he can respond to the language signals represented by patterns of auditory shapes" (p. 131).

John Downing's (1973) definition of reading is, for the purposes of cultural and language comparisons, ... "all that variety of behavior that people include in everyday life when they say that someone is reading" (p. 35). Any definition of reading can be criticized, but most reading teachers would include comprehension in their concept of reading.

Pronouncing words without understanding is not decoding. It is recoding from print that is not understood to speech that is not understood. In order to have an operational definition of reading as it is thought of in the elementary school curriculum, the following definition is suggested. Reading is a meaningful response to printed words that is appropriate to the author's intent. According to this definition, there is no reading without comprehension. A parrotlike pronunciation of words is often referred to as word-calling or barking at words. An activity that has children making speech sounds when they look at letters is much less rewarding than is making meaningful responses to print.

Reading a written message is really quite different from listening to spoken language. Children learn early in their school career that written language is different from the way people talk. This is one of the reasons that written language can be read successfully by speakers of various dialects. Speech includes pitch, stress, juncture, gestures, and facial expressions that are not as precisely signalled in writing. Written language makes use of a less familiar and more complex syntax with punctuation marks, paragraph indentations, and illustrations than is found in speech.

Durkin (1981) has explained that the difference between spoken and written language does not support Fries' (1962) contention that reading ability is no more than the ability to comprehend spoken language plus the ability to decode. These differences also "raise a question about the related contention that the only new task for beginners in reading is to learn to translate words into their spoken equivalent" (p. 31).

Reading is Reading

No matter how logical or sophisticated our definition of reading, we cannot observe the mental processes that actually go on in the reader's head. Whatever mental processes occur between word stimulus and meaning response are unseen processes of the mysterious "black box" (so called because we can't observe what's going on inside the person's head). We can, however, speculate on the nature of the intervening variables of the "black box".We can describe hypothetical constructs and then teach as though these constructs operate as we have described. Learning and intelligence are such constructs. Attitude, self-concepts, and mental imagery are constructs.

The success of psychoanalysis lends validity to the constructs of regression, repression, fixation, and other constructs of Freudian theory. Hypothetical constructs merely describe the processes and qualities that seem to help explain some of the mysteries of that unknown area between input stimulus and observable response. The more we attempt to analyze the reading process, the more complex and mysterious it seems.

Reading, although a meaningful response to printed words, is also a mysterious mental process that somehow stimulates thinking in response to abstract visual symbols. Printed words catalyze a synthesis of percepts into meanings and descriptions similar to those that the author would intend. Readers, however, do not try to analyze mental processes as they read. Reading is done only to satisfy a purpose. People read for information and enjoyment without regard for hypothetical constructs or mental processes. The reader simply searches through print for ideas and information when reading to satisfy a personal purpose.

Basic Reading Tasks

Whatever mental processes are involved with reading, there would seem to be three basic tasks:

1. Meaning identification: the ability to respond to the
   printed words with understanding of what the author
   intended to communicate. Or, finding out what you want to

know.

2. **Word identification**: the ability to associate the spoken form of the word with its printed counterpart for which the meaning is already known. and

3. **Oral reading**: the pronunciation of printed words with the voice dynamics of fluent speech.

Principle of Automaticity

The principle of automaticity of skill performance suggests that whenever two or more skills are performed at the same time, only one of these skills can be attended to while the other skills must be automatic. In other words, a person can attend to only one skill at a time. If a reader is identifying words and meaning at the same time, as would be required in silent reading, one of the two skills involved must be automatic. Identification of meaning must always be an active, conscious process that cannot occur automatically. The skilled reader must be able to identify words automatically in order to be able to attend to the meaning getting process. If the reader is thinking while reading and is trying to understand the author's message, he or she cannot be consciously aware of the application of word identification techniques.

Reading for meaning involves a process of digging down below the surface structure, the print, in order to get at the deep structure. Deep structure refers to the meaning intended by the author. We tend to skip over those words that don't help us to get the meaning when we are reading efficiently. Perhaps you can remember having learned a new word that later appeared to you in your reading material. The word existed before you learned its meaning but you didn't respond to it until it had value for signalling meaning. Herein lies the main value of direct vocabulary study; to make one aware of the existence and the meaning of words so that the new words will not be ignored, but will be confronted in a variety of contexts.

Reading Aloud Involves Three Tasks

When the reader is responsible for reading a passage aloud with the expression of fluent speech, word identification will precede pronunciation of the words. While silent reading requires only the identification of meaning with a minimum of information from specific words, oral reading requires accurate and specific identification of individual words so that they can be pronounced in a specific order for the benefit of the listeners.

The fluent oral reader would probably not listen to what was pronounced in order to understand what was read. In order to perform a fluent and accurate oral reading of a text, as is required by a radio or television announcer, the conscientious reader would preread the material silently in order to understand the message. Previous understanding of the meaning would then relieve the oral reading from the task of identifying meaning while giving attention to vocal expression and word pronunciation.

Asking a child to read orally upon sight, material that the child has not previously read silently, is asking for three tasks to be performed at the same time. As it is upon what the listeners hear that the oral reading performance is evaluated, the reader's primary and immediate task is to pronounce the words correctly and in the right order. In order to pronounce the words correctly, the fluent reader would normally be silently identifying four or five words ahead of the pronunciation when reading aloud (Levin and Turner, 1966). The fluent reader must attend to the identification of meaning in order to determine the word pronunciation and voice dynamics. The reader wouldn't know whether to pronounce read with a short or a long vowel without first knowing its contextual usage.

Oral reading of unstudied materials, therefore, puts an immediate extra burden upon the reader who must do everything that would be required for silent reading in addition to pronouncing the words in the correct order. When silent reading is the task, there is no demand upon the reader to identify specific words nor even to be aware of the surface structure. The only task in silent reading is to get through it and arrive at the meaning. Children who have not developed adequate skill in the three tasks of reading aloud tend to feel threatened by the requirement to read orally. The negative effect of such a threat, in the name of an activity that we want them to love, will depend upon the extent to which errors are accepted in the classroom situation as a normal part of the learning activity and upon the concept the child has of self as a reader and as an acceptable member of the group.   Oral reading, however, is a valuable learning activity for children that should be done in as nonthreatening an atmosphere as possible in order to avoid associating reading with unpleasantness. Just as easily as Pavlov's dog learned to salivate upon hearing a bell, failure-oriented, insecure children can quickly learn to hate reading under the fear of being called upon to read. Any instruction that teaches children to hate reading is worse than no instruction at all. It is important to building positive attitudes toward reading that reading activities are made to be as pleasant as possible for children.

Instruction in the subskills of reading, with little attention to meaning, has the inherent danger of teaching a wrong concept to children.   They may come to perceive reading as a difficult task that one does to please the teacher; or reading is marking in workbooks, or reading is being embarrassed by making pronunciation errors when reading aloud, or they may even learn that reading is "sounding out" words.   Teachers are cautioned to avoid an overemphasis on word analysis instruction that might cause young children to learn a wrong notion of the purpose and value of reading. The real reward from reading is not being able to identify words but to get meaning.

Sequence in Skills Learning

Fitz & Posner (1967) found the following sequence in their study of the development of skills:

1. Cognition: The learner has to know something about a skill. Pilots study in ground school before actually flying an airplane. Surgeons study about the human body before practicing with the scalpel. A clarinetist or pianist needs to learn where to put their fingers to produce each note. And children need to know some basics about reading before they actually begin doing it. Some of these readiness learnings will be explained later.

2. Stimulus-response conditioning: Commonly known as practice. Practicing the skill reduces resistance at the nerve connec-

tions so that impulses pass more freely along neural paths. Each time a child analyses a word for mediated identification makes it easier to identify the next time. This is what is meant by "practice makes perfect" and the recommendation that children "learn to read by reading".

3. <u>Automaticity</u>: With enough practice, the skill can be performed without conscious effort. When the skilled automobile driver comes to a stop sign, the foot goes to the brake pedal without thinking about where the brake pedal is or about how much pressure to put on it.

If we think of word identification as a skill or as the application of subskill, then we would expect a fluent reader to go through these three stages. We must help the learner to acquire the knowledge necessary to read; then encourage and provide for conditions in which to <u>practice</u> and keep on practicing to the point of automaticity. We might consider the automaticity stage to have been reached for each word that can be identified immediately, without analysis. One cannot read smoothly and attend to meaning while concentrating on word analysis. It's like trying to rub your stomach in a circular motion while patting your head.

SUMMARY

It was explained that phonics is only one of several strategies for mediating the identification of words and that word identification is only a means to meaning identification.
The teacher needs to learn about word identification techniques and linguistic principles to serve as a consultant for those children who may need some of this information.

Functional phonic knowledge is essential for good reading but is not necessarily acquired from doing a lot of phonic exercises. Too much attention to the subskills of reading may give the learner the impression that reading is "sounding out words" rather than a useful skill for acquiring information or for enjoying a story.

Reading was defined as a meaningful response to printed words that is appropriate to the author's intent. Pronouncing words without any attention to meaning is referred to as <u>word calling</u>. Written language is different from the way people talk. " There are three ways to spell too" can be spoken but cannot be written.

Reading involves three basic tasks and since one cannot attend to more than one task at a time, word identification must become automatic so that the learner is going to be able to attend to meaning. Skills seem to develop in a universal sequence of three stages 1) cognition, 2) stimulus-response conditioning, and 3) automaticity. If reading is a skill, then we must not skip nor minimize any of these stages of skill development. Children need to develop word identification skill to the point of automaticity in order to attend to the task of getting the rewards from reading; meaning.

References

Downing, J. (Ed.). (1973). Cross-national studies of behavior and processes in reading and writing. New York: Macmillan.

Durkin, D. (1981). What is the value of the new interest in reading comprehension? Language Arts, 58, 23-43.

Elkonin, D.B. (1973). USSR. In J. Downing, (ed.), Comparative reading: Cross-national studies of behavior and processes in reading and writing (pp. 551-579). New York: Macmillan.

Fitz, P. & Posner, M. (1967). Human performance, Belmont, California: Brooks Cole.

Fries, C. C. (1963). Linguistics and reading. New York: Holt, Rinehart & Winston.

Levin, H., & Turner, E.A. (1966). Sentence structure and the eye-voice span. Project literacy reports. Ithaca, New York: Cornell University, 7, 79-87.

STUDY GUIDE QUESTIONS

1. Describe the principle of automaticity of skill performance in your own words; illustrate with two examples of complex skills other than reading.

2. How might an overemphasis on phonics lead children into a misconception of the reading process?

3. What is the purpose for helping beginners to learn a few whole words before beginning phonic analysis?

4. What is the difference between recoding and decoding?

5. What would your definition of reading have been before you read the one in the book?

6. What is different about written language and speech?

7. List five hypothetical contructs that are not mentioned in this chapter.

8. Why can't a reader read for meaning while mediating the identification of words?

———————

CHAPTER II

WORD IDENTIFICATION CONCEPTS

When children are learning to read and are associating the printed words with the appropriate spoken words and their meanings, reading teachers refer to this activity as <u>word identification</u>, <u>word analysis</u>, or <u>word recognition</u>. In order to identify a word, a child must be able to associate the pronunciation of a word with its visual form. One might be able to recognize a word as one that has been seen before even though it can't be identified. The difference between word recognition and word identification is analogous to the difference between person recognition and person identification. In order to <u>recognize</u> someone, we must have seen them before. In order to <u>identify</u> a person, you must be able to name them. You may see someone coming down the street that you recognize but you can't think of their name. The same thing can happen to children when they are trying to identify a word. They know that they've seen it before but they just can't say it. If the printed word is one that can be identified without analyis, that is, the pronunciation of the word pops into the child's head as soon as it is seen, it has been identified immediately. This process is referred to as <u>immediate word identification</u>. All of the printed words that an individual can identify immediately, without analysis, are collectively referred to as that individual's <u>sight vocabulary</u>. A person's sight vocabulary includes all of those printed words that one can identify immediately, without analysis. When a printed word must be analyzed in order to be identified, we refer to the process of figuring out the spoken counterpart of the word as <u>mediation</u>. We teach children to use a variety of mediation techniques or strategies in order to identify printed words that they would be able to recognize if presented in their spoken form.

Teachers do not expect children to learn to identify printed words that they would not recognize in their spoken form. If we did expect children to pronounce a printed word that they didn't have in their understanding vocabulary, we would be asking them to <u>recode</u> the word from an unknown printed form, or code, into an unknown spoken code. The process of mediated word identification, therefore, is commonly referred to as <u>decoding</u> from an unknown printed word to a spoken form that is already known to the child. To teach a child to "sound out" the word <u>circus</u> is a meaningless exercise for the child who has no concept of a circus.

Terms and concepts involved with word identification can be very confusing and perhaps not as interesting as some of the other topics that you will study in the area of reading education. If you find word identification terms and concepts boring, use this feeling to empathize with the young child to whom you have assigned workbook pages on phonics.

Sugar Coating the Drill Pill

A child seldom finds intrinsic pleasure in the processes involved with the identification of specific words. Pleasant, or at least acceptable, activities may be used for the purpose of helping the pupil to develop skill with mediated word identification strategies. But pleasure, if any, must come from gamelike activities; from the joy of accomplishment or mastery; or from learning something that helps to get meaning from what is read. The child may enjoy playing a word game or receiving attention, praise, or tokens for appropriate responses to word-learning tasks. The pleasure of word learning can be expected to come from the activities that are associated with the identification of words or from the rewarding consequences of having learned to identify words. Successful word identification is a means to a greater end; reading. Care must be taken not to let word learning become perceived, by the pupil, as reading.

Identification of individual words may not necessarily be an absolute prerequisite to the meaning-getting process. The use of contextual clues, syntax, and semantics can be a very powerful word-identification strategy. Words such as read, lead, and proceed are dependent upon contextual information for their identification.

The most satisfactory rewards from reading activities will result from the information obtained from actual reading; from comprehension. When a child enjoys the experience of living vicariously through the senses of a story character, the reading is relevant to her or his desires. A child may receive aesthetic enjoyment from the mental pictures elicited from reading a poem. Another rewarding type of information, obtainable from reading, explains how to do or construct something.

The Uniqueness of Words

The printed form of each word in our vocabulary is unique. Each word is different in graphic form from every other word. Select any word and you won't find another exactly like that one, because, if you do, you really have the same word. This line of reasoning may seem esoteric but, to a beginning reader, would might look a lot like world. Chicken could be confused with children; are, were, there, where, and here may appear to be similar to the confused beginner at reading. The task involved in building a sight vocabulary is to be able to notice the unique appearance of each word. What makes the word horse different from house? Right! That's easy for you to say because you know the letter-sound relationships and you can perceive and discriminate those visual features that make the difference. But the beginning word learner needs to learn to look at words in a special way in order to notice how each one differs from words that are similar in appearance.

As children are learning to read and to identify words, they need to develop some way to notice the uniqueness of each word in order to make an adequate initial perception of the visual form of the word (Oliver, 1967). The way in which a child perceives a word will play an important role in the efficiency with which the child is able to add that word to a personal sight vocabulary. Sometimes adults are mystified as to why a child is still having difficulty identifying a simple word like house even though it has been pronounced for them thirty times. Well, it may not be that the child has forgotten the word as much as it is that the child just didn't really see the word clearly any of the thirty times that it was pronounced to him or her.

Building a Perceptual Net

It might be useful to think of a child's ability to learn new words as the building of a perceptual net. Each word analysis factor that a child learns adds a strand to the net until it is tightly woven enough to catch, scrutinize, and hold unfamiliar words just as a fisherman or fisherwoman can catch and hold a fish in his or her net. Perhaps the learner notices about how long the word is. The shape may be noticed, with a sticky-up part (ascender) here and a sticky-down (descender) part there. If the child is learning the word fish and already knows the word dish and feather, the child may note that the word starts like

feather and ends like fish.   If the child knows letter-sound
relationships and hears the sounds within the spoken word <u>fish</u>,
then it just makes sense that fish should start with the letter
"f" and that it has the same letters that spell "-ish" in the
word <u>dish</u>.

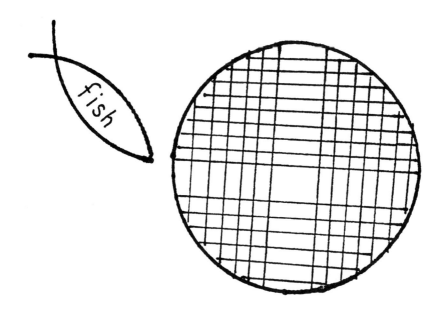

Perceptual Net

    Such a perceptual net will provide the beginning reader with
a tool to facilitate initial perception of newly presented words;
to really look at each new word, analyze it, visualize it, and
commit it to memory. The child will efficiently build a sight
vocabulary by dipping the perceptual net into a personal reservoir of word identification knowledge. Now the child is able to
make an adequate initial perception of the uniqueness of each new
word that is being added to a personal sight vocabulary.

If the learner's perceptual net is not tightly woven with strands of knowledge about letter-sound relationships, ability to segment language, and morphophonemic structures, the inadequately perceived word will slip away just as a fish would escape through a big enough hole in the fishnet. If the reservoir of word identification knowledge is deficient, the reader's initial perception of the word is apt to be too hazy to impress a clear mental image in his or her memory and the word will not be identified at sight upon the next encounter with it. A functional perceptual net will be used efficiently to quickly build the reader's fluency with oral reading as words are identified with a minimum of hesitation.

Visual Discrimination

How can you tell the difference between two bearded adult males who both wear glasses with wire frames and dress in suits and work at the same place that you work? Sometimes you don't discriminate between them and you say, "Good morning, Herman!" when you are really talking to Milt. So when you don't get the response that you were expecting, you take a closer look. You look for those visual characteristics that help you to identify Herman or Milt. Maybe it's the color or the look in their eyes that's different. Maybe you've noticed more gray in Herman's beard than in Milt's. It could be the difference in the shape of the nose, the height of the cheekbones, the curl of the mustache; or maybe it's just your perception of the aura of one or the other that's different. Milt might remind you of Kenny Rogers but Herman is like Errol Flynn. It could even have been that seeing one go into Milt's office gave you a clue. Whatever; somehow you know the difference when you take a closer look. You might not even be aware of how you know the difference between Herman and Milt. You just know! And the better you know both Herman and Milt, the less likely you are to mistake one for the other; the easier it is to notice what makes Milt's appearance unique and different from Herman's appearance. Even though Milt and Herman may have features that differ only slightly, each has features that you identify as making him unique in appearance. Those features that make it possible to identify Milt and Herman are distinctive.

Distinctive Features of a printed word are those visual features that enable a person to notice how that word is unique in appearance. The more experience that a person has at identifying a given word and the more that a person knows about words, and the context in which the word appears, the easier it is to identify a specific word. Distinctive features, or unique characteristics of words, are personal to some extent. Of course each word is spelled differently from every other word; but those features, of any particular word, that enable an individual to notice that word's unique appearance are, to a large extent, personal. I don't know how you distinguish Milt from Herman, and you may not know how I can tell the difference. (Actually, I don't even know anyone named Herman. The names are entirely fictional and used only for purposes of illustration.) Neither of us may even be aware of how we ourselves can tell the difference. A feature of a printed word that is distinctive for one person may not be distinctive for another. The more one knows about word identification techniques, however, the more information one has from which to select those features that make each word personally distinctive in appearance.

Teachers can provide opportunities for children to build feature lists by presenting words in pairs for comparison and by giving direct instruction in word identification techniques such as phonics. The main value of phonics is probably not to enable one to "sound out" words as much as it is to enable them to use letter-sound relationships to build a sight vocabulary by noting the unique apparance of each word.The way that words are spelled, orthography, makes sense to a person who knows the common letter-sound relationships and who hears the significant speech sounds within the spoken words that are represented by the print. Without a knowledge of common letter-sound relationships and the ability to perceive the significant sounds within spoken words, there is no rhyme nor reason to the way that words are spelled. In other words, orthography is rational to the child who perceives and discriminates phonemes and who has learned grapheme-phoneme coreespondences. Phonics is of no value in word identification for the child to whom spelling makes no sense.

Learning Words

There are different clues to word pronunciation. Visual clues are from the ink marks themselves. Other clues come from predicting a limited number of words that would make sense and would sound right in a particular context. As we read, we form alternative hypotheses about anticipated meanings. We make

predictions about the meaning to come from what we have read up
to that point. We use the visual information, printed words, to
support or reject our hypotheses. The less able we are to use a
hypothesis testing activity, the more that we must rely upon the
print. The more we know about grammar and the meanings intended
by the author, the less we need to rely on printed words.   In
other words, the more accurate our predictions, as we read, the
less print we need as evidence to support them.   Young children,
who are just learning to read, must rely much more upon the printed words in order to arrive at meaning than do older people who
are more aware of grammatical structure, writing styles, and
knowledge that comes from experience. Word identification techniques commonly recognized by teachers include:

Sight vocabulary
Phonic analysis
Structural analysis
Syntax
Semantics
Dictionary clues   (Diacritical Marking System)

Other techniques commonly used by children are guessing (prediction) and skipping. When reading for meaning, a person uses
information gained from a sample of the printed words. If a
printed word is not known, it must be guessed from use of context
clues according to what makes sense and sounds right in that
position. If the unknown word does not give any information, the
reader is likely to skip or ignore it.   Such a procedure is a
much more efficient way to read than to get hung up on unknown
words.

Sight Vocabulary

All of those words that a child can identify without analysis
make up the child's <u>sight vocabulary</u>. Because analyzing words
takes time and effort away from meaning identification, only
those words that can be identified immediately can be efficiently
read. The main value of phonic and structural analysis is in
building the sight vocabulary. Teachers do not expect instantan-
eous identification of words that are not in the child's meaning
or understanding vocabulary. It is important that children know
the meaning of words that they are expected to commit to their
sight vocabularies. As the child builds a storehouse of instantly recognized words, the child is also building reading ability.
The greater the sight vocabulary, the less need the child will

have to analyze words, and the more efficiently the child can read. Much of the building of sight vocabulary comes from responding to words in meaningful context; in other words, from actual reading.

Basic Sight Words

There is another common use of the term <u>sight vocabulary</u> among reading teachers that does not mean all of those words that a child can identify instantly without analysis. This other meaning refers to words that children must be able to identify without analysis in order to read efficiently. These <u>basic sight words</u>, service, or function words are so common, that no child will be able to read smoothly until these words can be identified immediately. Think about how it would slow a person down to have to "sound out" <u>and</u> or <u>the</u>. I have met children with such an obedient reverence for phonic analysis that it opened up a whole new world of reading enjoyment for them to discover that it was not cheating to just go ahead and pronounce <u>the</u> without sounding it out. One of the great dangers of an overemphasis on phonics instruction is that children may get the wrong idea about what reading is. I've often observed young children playing school at home. When they play "reading" period, they make strange sounds and contort their faces as though using phonics. Even teachers who are disciples of phonic analysis and talking letters permit children to learn the basic sight words without analysis. There are several lists of basic sight words but <u>the</u> and <u>and</u> appear on all of them.

Edward Dolch (1948) examined basal reader textbooks to identify the most commonly used words. Those appearing the most often are called high-frequency words or service words. Of the various high-frequency word lists, the Dolch Basic Sight Vocabulary has been the best known.

Otto and Chester (1972) identified 500 third-grade words and rank ordered them for frequency of occurrence. They call their list The Great Atlantic and Pacific Word List. An advantage of the Great A & P List is that any preferred number of words can be selected as the most frequently appearing words in third grade materials. A teacher who prefers 220 sight words may select the first 220; or only 100 of the most commonly used words may be selected.

Edward Fry (1980) updated his Instant Word List based on a

frequency count of 5,088,721 running words from 500-word samples taken from 1,045 different books in 12 subject matter areas used in grades three through nine. Fry claims that these words are appropriate for beginning readers of any age and that they make up 65% of all words in any textbook, newspaper, or magazine that is written in English.

Basic sight word lists can be useful in testing children for their ability to recognize them in isolation. Basal reader textbook authors refer to them as guidelines in vocabulary control. But be careful about spending a lot of time and energy trying to get children to learn the sight words from flash cards.

Teaching Service Words

Basic sight words, often referred to as _service_ words or _function_ words are usually short and difficult to associate with meaning. They are best learned in meaningful content. It is easier to identify the word _under_ in the phrase, _under the tree_, than it is to identify it in isolation. Although the identification of the word _under_ could be mediated with phonic analysis and auditory blending, few of the basic sight words are pronounced the way we would expect from their spelling. We should expect _said_ to rhyme with _paid_. The vowel-consonant-e (VCe) pattern in the word _have_ would be expected to rhyme with _save_. So, once again, the recommendation for teaching basic sight words to children is to get them to read connected discourse.

Flashing Isolated Words

Here is an easy trap of faulty logic to fall into. I did it myself. It goes like this: Most of the running words in books used for elementary school children are found on a basic sight word list. These words make up a large percentage of the running words that children will read. Children can never read smoothly if they are going to stumble on words that appear so frequently in what they read. Therefore; children must learn to identify the basic sight words in isolation before they are ready to read them in context. Be careful with such logic. I tried this in my own remedial reading class. What a waste of time! I had it so well planned. I had the rationale worked out on the basis of operant conditioning and reinforcement theory. I sent for the Dolch Basic Sight Words and Fry's Instant Word List on filmstrips. I got a slide projector and an expensive tachistiscope.

I made up a record sheet with the pupils names along the side and sections of sight words along the top so that I could check pupils off as they demonstrated performance. I presented the words, individually, to pupils at timed tachistiscopic exposures of 1/10th, 1/25th, 1/50th, and finally 1/100th of a second. It was in the Spring of the school year and I wanted my remedial readers to really know these words at mastery level before Summer vacation came. I wanted them to be able to read during Summer vacation and get a head start for Fall. I want to tell you, I was really proud of these kids. They all got checked-off on all of these little words at 1/100th of a second exposure. I really felt good about this accomplishment!

Basic Sight Words are Best Learned from Reading Books

I checked on them after Summer vacation. They had forgotten the words that they had mastered in the Spring. I couldn't believe it. But maybe there was some sort of a memory trace in their long term memory that could be accessed later. Maybe. But I did learn two things from this experience: (1) When they could identify a word at 1/10th of a second, they could identify it at 1/100th. There seemed to be a lingering retinal image from the brief exposure such that each word was perceived regardless of the exposure time, and (2) Exposing children to words in isolation is an inefficient use of time and energy. I reversed my thinking. Experience with teaching elementary children to identify service words suggests that a strategy just the opposite of that explained above will be expected to be much more productive in helping children learn to identify basic sight words. If children's books are written such that most of the words contained in them are service words, then why not let children read the books? While reading books, over half of the words children will respond to in meaningful content are the service words. The words are in context with clues to their use and identification. Children seem to learn basic sight words more efficiently in meaningful context than they do in isolation.

Partner Reading

I tried this new logic on my remedial readers and it was great. I purchased many children's books in paperback and duplicated several lists of them. On each list I put two children's names. The two children were partners for reading. I had to select partners who would work well together. I gave each pair a paperback book to read. The task was for the partners to take turns reading a page aloud. The child on the left reads the page on the left while the partner listens and offers to help with word identification if asked. Then they reverse tasks while the child on the right reads the page on the right aloud. If they come to a word that neither of them knows, they can raise a hand and the teacher will pronounce the word that is above the pointing finger. I would circulate around the table listening to children read aloud. I carried a clipboard with the record-sheets on it. Each record sheet had both partners names on it. Whenever a book was completed, a child would hold it up and I would trade it for one that they hadn't yet read. I would circle the title of the book that was completed. Now I could tell at a glance who had read which books. In a fifty-minute session, each pair of children would have read two or three books. They were small books like Nobody Listens to Andrew, Bread and Jam for Francis, The Boy Who Wouldn't Say His Name, and Clifford, The Big Red Dog, but the children were reading them. They were not only getting the stimulus-response conditioning for reinforcement of the service words, but they were enjoying the stories and the activity of reading together. There had to be rules though. Some partners would try to cheat by skipping pages; competition was high. We had to make a rule that partners caught skipping a page would have to go back to the beginning. That worked. When I retested them on their sight words, they knew them again in isolation, but I feel that most of their learning took place from reading the books rather than from the tachistiscopic exposure.

SUMMARY

Word identification is the ability to pronounce a printed word while recognition is knowing that it has been seen before. A person's sight vocabulary is composed of words that can be identified without mediation. Children decode words by arriving at the pronunciation of a printed word for which they already know the meaning. Drill on word identification activities can be made into games that lead painlessly to achievement. The real rewards from reading are those that come from enjoying a story or obtaining some desired information. The more children learn about the characteristics of words, the more efficiently they can build feature lists for perceiving the unique appearance of each word.

Clues to word identification are visual or non-visual. Young children need to rely on visual clues until they know more about

grammar and have more life experience. The less non-visual information that children can use to identify words by prediction,
the more visual information they must use. Children will build
their sight vocabularies more efficiently from actual reading
than they will from studying words in isolation.

References

Dolch, E. (1948). Problems in reading. Champaign, Illinois:
Garrard Press.

Fry, E. (1980). The new instant word list. The Reading Teacher,
34, 284-289.

Oliver, M.E. (1967). Initial perception of word forms.
Elementary English, 44, 383-385.

Otto, W. & Chester, R. (1972). Sight words for beginning
readers. Journal of Educational Research, 65, 435-443.

STUDY GUIDE QUESTIONS

1. Explain the difference between a basic sight word list
   and a personal sight vocabulary.

2. What misperception might a child form if required to spend
   too much time and effort in mediated word identification
   activities?

3. How could a child forget a word that has been presented
   many times?

4. Why can't children be taught feature lists for specific
   words?

5. What makes orthography rational for a beginning reader?

6. Name four mediated word identification techniques or four
   strategies for figuring out what a new word is.

7. How are basic sight words most efficiently learned?

8. What is another name for <u>service words</u>?

9. How many words should a child be able to identify before being allowed to read books?

10. What percentage of running words in English would be expected to appear on Fry's Instant Word List?

CHAPTER III

Linguistics and Phonics

Linguistics is the scientific study of language. Psycholinguistics combines psychology and linguistics to study areas such as language acquisition, how people learn to read, and the reading process. As scientists, linguists and psycholinguists are more concerned with truth than with teaching children to read. They would caution teachers, however, to learn the truth about letter-sound relationships no matter what kinds of stories teachers tell in order to help children learn to read.

Do Letters Talk?

While teachers are more concerned with helping children learn to read than they are with linguistic science, it can be very helpful for teachers to know some of the linguistic properties of language. For instance, even though a teacher might ask a child, "What sound does this letter make?" or "What does 'b' say?" the teacher should know that letters do not "make" nor "have" sounds; nor do they talk. Letters, or graphemes as linguists call them, spell, signal, or represent speech sounds.

Phonemics, Phonetics, and Graphemes

Linguists refer to significant sounds within words as phonemes. Reading teachers commonly use this term also to refer to the smallest significant unit of speech of a particular language. But what makes a speech sound significant? Nonsignificant sound differences are illustrated by the different sound represented by the letter "d" in dog, older, and bad. These subordinate sounds are called allophones. Allophones sound the same to us because the slight differences in their sound is not significant. The phoneme represented by the letter "d" includes a range of allophones. The study of phonemes is called phonemics. Phonemes are functional speech sounds which contrast in the same environment. In bad and dad, the initial consonants /b/ and /d/ contrast in the same environment; that is, at the beginning of the word, followed by the same vowel. Therefore /b/ and /d/ are phonemes because they pass the test. Phonemes are the smallest significant units of speech in a particular language. A phonemic difference makes a difference in meaning . Therefore phonemes are psychological categorizations of speech sounds. Every language has between 30 and 50 phonemes. English has between 35 and 45, depending on how they are counted. For instance, some people might count the /a/ in father as phonemically different from the sound represented by the letter "o" in octopus, while others would categorize them as allophones of the same phoneme. A popular phoneme count for teachers seems to be 44.

Counting Phonemes for the Reading Teacher

Graphemes are used to represent, or signal, phonemes. A simplified definition of a grapheme is that a grapheme is a letter or that graphemes are letters. Such a definition, while easy to remember, may mislead one in counting phonemes. The difficulty in counting phonemes seems to come from the tendency to superimpose a visual image of the written word, the spelling, over the sound that we hear and then to count the letters.

If we hear someone pronounce "ox" we may visualize the spelling and count two letters, but there are three significant sounds in "ox" (/ah/ + /k/ + /s/). The one letter "x", in this case, represents two phonemes. In other words, such as xylaphone, the letter "x" represents only one phoneme /z/.

Sometimes more than one letter can represent a phoneme. The letters in the consonant digraph "ng" represent one phoneme in the word "sing" but two phonemes in the word "finger". The digraph "th" may spell different phonemes as in "this, Thimble, and Thames.

Practice counting phonemes in the following words by:

1. Pronouncing them

2. Listening for the significant sounds one at a time

3. Pronounce the word without the sound identified as significant

4. Try to break that sound down into smaller significant speech units

5. Look at the answers on page 36 only after you have made your count. Do not count syllables as phonemes. If you have studied linguistics or phonetics you may not agree with the answers which are most appropriate for reading. A diphthong counts as a single phoneme in reading. A diphthong is the vowel represented by the "oi" in "oil" or the "ow" in "cow".

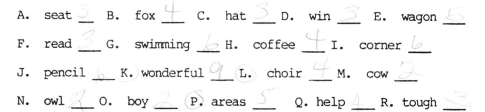

A. seat ___   B. fox ___   C. hat ___   D. win ___   E. wagon ___

F. read ___   G. swimming ___   H. coffee ___   I. corner ___

J. pencil ___   K. wonderful ___   L. choir ___   M. cow ___

N. owl ___   O. boy ___   P. areas ___   Q. help ___   R. tough ___

Phonetics is the scientific study of all perceptible differences among speech sounds and how they are produced. Linguists use brackets to enclose phonetic symbols; [p], and slanted lines to enclose phonemic symbols; /p/. Speech differences that are phonemic in one language, because they are significant (can make a difference in meaning) may be phonetic in another language. Phonetic differences in words have no relationship to the spelling and are therefore, of little value for the identification of printed words. Letters that spell phonemes are called graphemes. When we teach phonics, we teach children to associate speech sounds with the letters that spell those sounds. To teach phoneme–grapheme relationships implies that the learner will be able to perceive these associations within words. Phonemes cannot be pronounced in isolation from the word in which they belong. Attempts to do so produce distorted sounds.

Phoneme perception is a prephonics skill. Although children can learn phonics without perceiving phonemes, they will be unable to apply their knowledge of phonics to mediate the identification of printed words. Phoneme perception is a prerequisite to word identification. Carroll (1960) indicated that 90 percent of the children entering school correctly produce all but seven of the phonemes of English. Elkonin (1973) reported Shvatchkin's finding that the child is able to distinguish words that differ from one another by a single phoneme as early as two years of age. Obviously a very young child would have little difficulty discriminating between candy and dandy or between dandy, Randy, and brandy. But to discriminate words that are alike or different is a much lower level of difficulty than to discriminate between words that begin or end with the same sound. Example: Which of the following words begins like apple? (Teacher pronounces the following words): athlete, elbow, silver, astronaut.

Both perceptions, described above, are classified under the general term of auditory discrimination but the categorizing of words by beginning, middle, and ending sounds requires greater segmentation of the language than does the categorization of spoken words as alike or different.

Durrell (1971) reported that one-fourth of the children entering first grade can identify about half of the phonemes; another one-fourth cannot demonstrate that they even discern phonemes at all; and half of the beginners can identify about fourteen beginning sounds within words. Murphy and Durrell (1965) have a subtest for phoneme perception in their Murphy-Durrell Reading Readiness Analysis.

Surface and Deep Structure of Language

A thought, feeling, idea, or mental picture that is to be communicated is in the form of deep meaning or deep structure. A writer encodes that deep structure into a string of words and punctuation marks called surface structure that is seen by the reader as printed words. The writer has control over the surface structure in the way he or she strings the words together. The reader's task is much more difficult than is the writer's. The reader must speculate on the deep meaning and withhold closure while considering alternate meanings. Closure doesn't come until after confirming a deep structure from processing available visual data. Comedians are very skillful at arranging words in such a way that the audience is tempted to accept, without sufficient data, a deep structure that becomes ridiculous or bizarre upon presentation of more conclusive data referred to as the punch line.

The quality and extent of an imaginative communication depends upon two basic factors:

(1) the ability of the author to arrange the surface structure in such a way as to elicit a response, by the reader, in terms of mental images, emotions, ideas, and thoughts like those of the writer, and

(2) the ability of the reader to respond to the stimulus words with mental images, emotions, ideas, and thoughts like those of the writer.

Using Picture and Configuration Clues

Pictures can be helpful for identifying words. Children, in a sense, read the pictures. Traditional basal reader text primers usually present most of the story through pictures. Although pictures present no linguistic clues, they are clues to meaning which may reduce linguistic alternatives. Some educators feel that pictures should not be used as a "crutch" to identify words. "Linguistic" basal readers avoid using picture clues in order to restrict attention to word forms. There is no evidence that the use of picture clues is detrimental to learning to read or to identify words. Pictures really add to the context. Very young pre-primary children often use the sense of the environment to guess the meaning of labels. If the door at the super market opens in, then a young learner might guess that the word on the door is "in". When it opens out, the word guessed might be "out". Sometimes they can guess wrong. The child might guess that the sign in the window at Taco Time reads "Taco Time" when it actually says "Help Wanted". But the point is that young children do try to guess what the words spell in their environment by what makes the most sense. They have the right idea but need to learn some other word identification techniques in combination with context or pictures.

Some beginning instructional materials use <u>rebus</u> pictures to replace words. A rebus is not a picture clue. It is just used to replace a word; usually a noun.

Picture clues merely reduce alternatives to meaning. They are not precise. The child cannot tell whether the word form is Daddy, Father, or man from the picture. The guess needs to be confirmed by other word identification techniques or by someone who knows the word form.

Visual configuration clues refer to those physical characteristics of printed words that can serve as <u>distinctive features</u> for the reader who notices or uses them as clues. They include such things as word length, shape, the nature of the upper or lower half of the word with ascenders and descenders. Ascenders are the "sticky-up" letters and descenders are the "sticky-down" letters. The upper half (coastline) of printed words seems to provide more useful clues to word identification than the lower coastline does. Cover the lower half of a line of print and you will find that the line is much more readable than when you cover the upper half. Capital letters, used to spell proper nouns and Mom and Dad can help some readers identify names. But remember, configuration clues are only useful in identifying words for the person who notices and uses them as distinctive features; a personal choice. A visual configuration that is useful for one person may not be for another. It is questionable how useful it would be to try to teach visual configuration clues. Get the pupil to read and those clues that make a difference will emerge as significant personal clues to word identification.

Semantic and Syntactic Context Clues

Individual words are difficult to identify in speech. There is often a greater length of pause within words than between words. It is especially difficult to identify individual words in announcements on commercial airline takeoffs or in toothpaste commercials where the losers "Dint win but they gah'lah free toothpaste." Spoken words, like phonemes, are not discrete units of speech except by psychological categorization. Printed words, bounded by space, define spoken words as confirmed by the dictionary and convention or tradition. It is no wonder that children have difficulty segmenting speech into separate words when they are just beginning to learn to read. Teachers should avoid emphasis upon individual words. Although children need to learn to match written words with their spoken counterpart, meaning is signalled in context; not by individual words. Meaning must be emphasized from the very beginning of reading instruction even though beginners need so much visual information.

While beginners need to identify all of the words, skillful readers use a variety of word identification techniques in context; visual configuration or shapes of words, picture clues, semantic and syntactic clues and structural clues.

Context clues, or meaning, can be a primary word identification technique by helping learners to predict words in context. Semantic clues answer the question "does it make sense?" while syntactic clues answer the question "Does it sound right?" Context clues can also be used to confirm the accuracy of words that have been identified by other means. Semantics refers to meaning, to lexical information. Syntax has to do with grammatical information and word order in sentences. But the order of words affects meaning so that syntactic and semantic clues are interrelated in the identification of words.

The use of context clues is dependent on the reader's general knowlege, vocabulary, and awareness of the linguistic properties of language. The frame of reference is a context clue to meaning. The topic helps us to know whether bark is on a tree or on a dog. Such words as bark, lead, read, progress, etc. depend upon semantic clues for their identification.

Structural Analysis

Analysis of the morphological structure of words can be a useful word identification technique. A morpheme is the smallest spoken or written unit of meaning. Morphemes are not to be confused with syllables. A morpheme always represents meaning. A syllable is the unit of pronunciation and does not represent meaning. The /s/ (speech sound) or "s" (letter) on the word dogs is a morpheme since it represents the plural for dog. A morpheme may contain more than one syllable as in the word giraffe.

morphemes should also not be confused with phonemes. Although the word <u>oxen</u> is only one morpheme, it contains five phonemes.

In order to identify morphemic units, the learner must be familiar with roots (base words), prefixes, suffixes, and inflections.

<u>Roots</u> or <u>Base words</u>, sometimes referred to as the stem, signal the main part of the word's meaning. Free roots are always able to stand alone as real words and are called <u>free morphemes</u>. Affixes can be connected to base words to make derivitives and inflections. We are really only concerned with identifying free roots or bases in elementary school.

<u>Prefixes</u> are bound morphemes that are attached before the root or stem and serve to modify its meaning. The most effective way to teach identification of prefixes is to show pupils the base word and add the prefix to it such as like, unlike; do, undo; tie,untie, etc.

<u>Suffixes</u> are added to the end of roots to make <u>derivitives</u>. A derivitive, or derived word, is composed of a root plus a prefix, derivational suffix, or both. Suffixes are bound, like prefixes, because they cannot stand alone. Suffixes often indicate the part of speech and may also affect meaning. American is a derivitive of America and sailor is a derivitve of sail.

The function of derivational suffixes should be understood by reading teachers just so they'll know and be able to answer pupil's questions. It is not recommended that children be expected to learn about them.

<u>Inflections</u>, or <u>variants</u>, are words that have been modified to take on a new use such as a noun that has been made plural or possessive; an adjective or adverb that has been modified to past tense or participle. (A participle is a form of a verb that is used as an adjective or a noun) Endings that have these functions are called <u>inflectional endings</u>.

<u>Base</u>	<u>Inflection</u>	<u>Modification</u>
dog	s	dogs
perch	es	perches
candy	(change y to i and ad es)	candies
tape	d	taped
tap	ped	tapped

<u>Compound words</u> are formed from combinations of free mor-

phemes.

(cup + cake = cupcake; base + ball = baseball, etc)

Syllabication

Syllables are units of pronunciation. There is considerable disagreement among reading authorities as to whether it is worthwhile to teach syllabication rules. Some point out that it is just too difficult to mediate the identification of polysyllables through the application of rules. Linguists, generally reject the value of teaching syllabication rules for word identification. Phonics, however, cannot be applied to polysyllables. The separate syllables need to be identified before phonics can be useful. Most reading teachers do, however, agree on the value of teaching students the open-closed syllable rule as explained below.

Sometimes, even students who are very good at identification of words throughout elementary grades, begin to have considerable difficulty with the heavy polysyllabic vocabulary load when they begin junior high school. Some instruction in a word pronunciation strategy for polysllables could be very helpful.

Basic Phonetic Understandings for Syllabication

1. There are two kinds of sounds with which people speak. All speech sounds may be categorized as either <u>vowels</u> or <u>consonants</u>. Vowels, produced with a minimum of audible friction, are referred to by reading teachers as <u>open</u> sounds. Vowels are produced with relatively free passage of air through open speech mechanisms.

   Consonants, produced with increased audible friction, are referred to by reading teachers as <u>closed</u> or <u>restricted</u> speech sounds. Consonants are produced by restricting or stopping the free passage of vibrating sound as air passes through the speech mechanisms. Vowels are <u>open</u> speech sounds. Consonants are <u>closed</u> or <u>restricted</u> speech sounds.

2. Syllables that end with consonants are called <u>closed</u> syllables. Syllables that end with <u>vowels</u> are called <u>open</u> syllables.

3. <u>Open</u> syllables usually have <u>long</u> vowel sounds.
   (Note that the use of the word "sounds" following vowel is

actually as superfluous as saying sugar before diabetes since vowels and consonants are actually "sounds", NOT letters. Teachers are urged to use this redundant strategy to clarify whether they are referring to vowels or letters that represent vowels.) <u>Closed</u> syllables are expected to have <u>short</u> vowels.

Basic Structural Analysis Rules

1. Divide compound words into simple words (free morphemes)

2. Remove prefixes and suffixes from base words.

3. Divide between consonants. (In VC/CV combinations)

4. Divide before a single consonant. (In V/CV combinations). The consonant letter "X" is an exception because it usually represents two consonant sounds.

5. The "le" on the end of a word should retain the consonant letter that comes before it to form a syllable in which the vowel is heard between the two consonants. i.e. (ta ble   ket tle   ter ri ble   syl la ble)

After the polysyllabic word has been divided, each syllable can be sounded out as a monosyllable. These syllables must then be synthesized into a word which is already within the understanding vocabulary of the reader by experimenting with a pronunciation which shifts the accent from one syllable to another until the spoken sound is recognized as a known word. This is kind of an ear-training exercise. As soon as the accent is taken from a syllable, its vowel becomes obscured and sounds about the same as it would if it were symbolized by any other vowel letter. The five rules above are not hard and fast but will serve as a guideline for analysis.

There is a vowel in every syllable and a syllable for every vowel.

The mouth <u>must</u> open in order to produce a vowel sound. Opening the mouth forces the jaw down one time for each syllable that is pronounced. Therefore; one can count the number of syllables in each spoken word by counting the number of times the jaw goes down when pronouncing it. Of course, you must pronounce the word

with a clear articulation.   It won't work for ventriliquists.
There is a kind of a rhythm to syllables too.   Children can learn
a sense of syllables in words by clapping to the rhythm along
with the teacher's lead.

PHONIC CONTENT

Phonics is the use of grapheme-phoneme relationships to mediate the identification of words.   Phonics is a useful word identification technique for the alphabetic writing system of English.
Phonics is commonly known to parents as "sounding-out" words
although the main value of phonic knowledge is really for the
efficient development of a sight vocabualary.   The more information the child has about phonics, the more equipped that child
will be to efficiently build a sight vocabulary.   The learner who
knows 1) grapheme-phoneme relationships, and who can 2) segment
spoken words into phonemic units can make sense of our spelling
system.   Linguists use the term, orthography, to refer to our
spelling system.

We use visual and non-visual information when reading.   The
visual information is the printed words and the non-visual information is what we know about our language and about the subject
that we are reading.   The more non-visual information that we
have, the less visual information we need and vice versa.   Beginning readers tend to rely very heavily on the visual information
and use context clues to confirm their pronunciations.   Better
readers need less visual information and so rely more on context
clues and use a minimum of phonics only to confirm their identification when necessary.   So the effective reading teacher
strives to wean the pupil away from a dependency on phonic analysis for word identification.   Meaning and context clues should
always be a more important objective than word pronunciation.

* * * * * * * * *

Answers to Counting Phonemes for the Reading Teacher (page 29)

A. 3	B. 4	C. 3	D. 3	E. 5	F. 3	G. 6
H. 4	I. 6	J. 6	K. 9	L. 4	M . 2	N. 2
O. 2	P. 5	Q. 4	R. 3			

NOTE: Each diphthong counts as one phoneme in reading.

Letters do not have sounds or make sounds. Letters represent, spell, or signal speech sounds. People produce the sounds. Considerable confusion about phonics can be avoided if the teacher will keep, clearly in mind, the difference between what is heard and what is seen. It should be kept in mind that speech is primary to print. The letters represent speech sounds.

Voiced and Unvoiced Phonemes for the Teacher of Reading

Some teachers find it very difficult to discriminate between voiced and unvoiced consonants. This is not something that you should attempt to teach to the child who is learning to read but it is important for the teacher to know in order to categorize words for a specific sound to minimize confusion in teaching. This is part of the content that reading teachers need to know.

Voiced speech sounds are produced by using the voice. In order to use our voice, our vocal folds (or cords or bands if you prefer) vibrate. We use our voice to produce all vowels. All vowels are voiced. But some consonants are unvoiced. We produce some consonant sounds without vibrating our vocal folds. The trick is to determine which ones are voiced and which ones are not.

The difference between the words bus and buzz is phonemic. The only difference in pronunciation of bus and buzz is that the voice is used at the end of buzz but not at the end of bus. Pronounce "bus" and hold onto the ending sound with your fingers on your neck. Notice that you feel no vibration as air hisses between your tongue and the ridge behind your upper teeth. Of course if you are just whispering the pronunciation of "bus", you won't use your voice for any part of it. Or if you put your fingers on your throat when you begin pronouncing bus, you'll feel the vibration from the pronunciation of the vowel in the medial position. Now, with your fingers still on your throat, pronounce "buzz" and prolong the ending sound. You should be able to discern a vibration in your throat. That little buzzing vibration makes the difference between the meaning of the words bus and buzz.

A. Pronounce the following words and determine in which ones you feel the vibration from the sound spelled by the letter "s". Circle the words containing the voiced "s" sound /z/.

has	class	Tuesday	kiss	readers	Sunday
is	sun	twins	was	sit	news

You should have circled has, Tuesday, readers, is, twins, was, and news.

B. In order to discriminate the voiced and unvoiced sounds commonly spelled with the letters "th", do the finger-on-the-throat technique for the ending sound of <u>bath</u> and <u>bathe</u>. Can you discern the vibration at the end of bathe? If not, keep trying. Try <u>tooth</u> and <u>toothe</u>. The spelling is a dead giveaway because many words have a <u>the</u> to spell the sound at the end of the word.

Some of the phonemes that reading teachers call "voiced consonants" such as /m/, /n/, and /ng/ may be referred to by phoneticians as <u>semi-vowels</u> but we want to simplify the terminology so we call these phonemes <u>voiced consonants</u>.

C. If you can feel the vibration at the end of <u>bathe</u> and <u>toothe</u>, pronounce each of the following words and circle those in which "th" or "the" represents a voiced sound.

breath	heather	thistle	breathe	lathe	this
thermos	Thursday	thimble	through	thigh	that
those	think	there	Thames	thy	them

<u>Answer</u>:   You should have circled: heather, breathe, lathe, this, that, those, there, thy, and them.

The <u>Glossary of Phonic and Linguistic Terms</u> that is presented on the next page is structured in a sequence that seems more logical for learning than an alphabetic order would be.

GLOSSARY OF PHONIC AND LINGUISTIC TERMS

Speech sounds: Communicative utterances produced by human
        mechanisms. Any speech sound may be categorized as a
        vowel or a consonant depending upon the amount of
        audible friction required for its production.

Consonant sound: A closed or restricted speech sound produced
        with more audible friction than is a vowel. Consonants
        and vowels are referred to, by reading teachers, as
        consonant sounds and vowel sounds so as to clarify
        reference to speech rather than to print (letters).

Consonant letter: A letter that represents (usually spells or
        signals) a consonant. Often referred to as "single
        consonants"; more accurately single consonant-letters.

Consonant blend: A fusion of two or more consonants in a word
        without loss of the sound represented by any of the
        single consonant-letters. Note that a blend is NOT a
        combination of letters.

Consonant cluster: Sometimes used as a synonym for consonant
        blend. More commonly used to refer to combinations of
        two or three letters that represent a consonant blend or
        "blend". Examples: The letters "bl" that represent /bl/
        in black or "str" to represent /str/ in street. NOTE:
        For the purposes of reading this glossary, quotations
        marks around letters refer to letters, while slash marks
        refer to the speech sounds represented by the letters.

Consonant digraph: Two letters that signal a consonant phoneme
        that is not usually spelled by either letter alone.
        "ch" in chop, but not in school. There are six pairs
        of letters that can be consonant digraphs: sh, ch,
        gh, ph, ng, & th. gh is a digraph in tough but not
        in ghost.

Consonant trigraph: Three letters that signal a consonant such
        as "tch" in pitch, catch, match, and watch. Note: The

digraph "ch" is always used to spell the /ch/ sound at the beginning of words. "tch" is always used to spell /ch/ at the end of words when /ch/ follows a short vowel with only five exceptions: **rich, such, much, which, and touch.**

Voiced consonants are produced by the vibration of the vocal folds. The significant difference between the pronunciation of bus and buzz is only the voicing of the final sound. The /th/ in the words thy, bathe, and breathe are voiced. NOTE: **All vowels are voiced.**

Voiceless consonants are produced without vibration of the vocal folds. The consonant associated with "th" in thigh, bath, and breath are unvoiced.

Soft c or g: The sound represented by these letters when they come before e, i, or y in words such as **city, cent, cymbal, giant, gem, & gypsy.**

Hard c or g: The sound represented by these letters when they come before a, o, or u in words such as **catalog, cost, cut, gate, gone, or gun.**

Vowel digraph: Two letters that spell one vowel such as a diphthong or "au" in caught, "aw" as in saw, and "oo" in cook or cool.

Diphthong: The vowel phoneme /ou/ as in out and /oy/ as in boy. Linguistically, a diphthong is produced by gliding two vowels together as in what reading teachers call the long sound represented by the "a" in cake or the "i" in hike. Can you find the three digraphs in the word diphthong? The diphthongs that reading teachers are concerned with are usually spelled with the vowel digraphs **oi, oy, ou, and ow,** and sometimes ough. But those digraphs don't always spell diphthongs, i.e. **tow, bow, sow.**

Short "oo": The sound represented by "oo" in such words as **book, took, look, good, and brook.**

Long "oo": The sound represented by "oo" in such words as **moon, food, school, pool, and tool.**

Short vowels: The sound represented by "a" in apple, "e" in elephant, "i" in image, "o" in ostrich and "u" in umbrella.

Long vowels: If letters could talk, their long sounds would be what people would hear when the letter says its own name. i.e. the /a/ in cake and race.

Phoneme: The smallest significant unit of speech in a specific language. Significant units of speech are those that make a difference in meaning in the same environment. For example: The beginning sound in "bad" makes the word's meaning different from " Dad"; Rake and Lake differ in only the beginning sound but make the meaning of the words different in English. They would not be significantly different in a language that did not consider /l/ and /r/ phonemic differences. There are about 44 phonemes in English.

Grapheme: A letter or combination of letters that represent a phoneme. NOTE: The use of the term graph- by linguists is usually in reference to print, as opposed to a record of light as in a photograph or a record of sound as in a phonograph record. Reading teachers and linguists both use the term graphic information in reference to printed words.

Phonics: A term used by reading teachers to refer to the use of grapheme-phoneme (letter-sound) relationshps to mediate word identification, or, as some say, to "decode" which actually may be recoding from print to speech.

Phonetics: The science of describing human speech.

Phonemics: The study of phonemes.

Linguistics: The scientific study of language.

Phonograms: Endings of words categorized into families. See Durrell, D. & Wiley.(October,1970). "Teaching vowels through phonograms". Elementary English, pp. 787-790. Phonograms stabalize vowel sounds. Nearly 500 primary grade words are derived from the following 37 phonograms:

-ack, -aw, -ain, -ake, -ame, -an, -ank, -ap, -ash, -at,

-ate, -aw, -ey, -eat, -ell, -est, -ice, -ick, -ide, -ight, -ill, -in, -ine, -ing, -ink, -ip, -it, -ock, -oke, -op, -ore, -ot, -uck, -ug, -ump, and -unk.

Rhyming words: Words that sound alike except for the initial sound., i.e. light, fight, kite. Fat rhymes with sat and cat but not with tap.

Schwa: An upside-down e used to represent the vowel in an unaccented syllable such as the vowel represented by the "o" in lemon, the "u" in circus, the "a" in about, and the "i" in pencil. Lemon is pronounced lem'n with an obscure (not clearly heard) sound between the /m/ and the /n/.
ə

TERMS COMMONLY USED IN SYLLABICATION AND PHONICS INSTRUCTION

Analytic phonics: A linguistic inductive method of teaching phonics. Analyzes specific commonalities of spoken words to help children discover their printed representation. Emphasizes a speech to print sequence and avoids the isolation of phonemes. Based on the premise that speech is primary. Preferred by linguists.

Synthetic Phonics: A deductive approach to phonics. Combines parts of words into whole words by auditory blending. Emphasizes a print-to-speech sequence based on the premise that print is primary. Would combine cuh-a-tuh into "cat". Preferred method of intensive phonics proponents.

Visual discrimination: The ability to identify likenesses and differences among printed words.

Auditory discrimination: The ability to hear likenesses and differences among spoken words.

Phonemic perception, or Phonematic hearing:
The ability to hear, perceive, and discriminate significant sounds within spoken words and to know that spoken words are constructed of combined speech sounds.

Phonic substitution is the minimal substitution of one grapheme in a member of a word group so that the pronunciation differs from the other members by only one phoneme. When only the initial phoneme is substituted, the words are said to <u>rhyme</u> with each other; i.e. fight, light.

<u>Syllable</u>: The unit of pronunciation of a word. Every syllable contains a vowel. For every vowel, there is a syllable.

<u>Open syllable</u>: A syllable that ends with a vowel. Open syllables usually have long vowels. (ta-, me-, go-).

<u>Closed syllable</u>: A syllable that ends with a consonant. A closed syllable is expected to have a short vowel. (tap, sit, dic-, -ing.)

<u>Word recognition</u>: The ability to recognize a word as one that has been seen before, just as one can recognize a person as one who has been seen before.

<u>Word identification</u>: The ability to pronounce a word or to identify a printed word in response to its pronunciation.

Other reading pedagogical terms:

<u>Basal Reading Series</u>: A set of graded textbooks designed to present a systematic, comprehensive, and sequential development of alleged reading subskills that have been operationally defined via a scope and sequence chart.

<u>Linguistic Basal Series</u>: A basal reading series called "linguistic" because the origin of their format was recommended by structural linguists, Charles Fries & Leonard Bloomfield. They begin with the naming of letters. Children analyze and induce phonic generalizations about letter-sound correspondences. Vocabulary is controlled by the introduction and repetition of spelling patterns, beginning with the most frequent CVC as in Mat is a fat cat. Nan can fan Dad and Dan with a bad fan. Context and picture clues are minimized.

<u>Word</u>: (Printed) A group of letters bounded by space and occupying a single entry in the dictionary. (Spoken) When such a word is pronounced, it is a spoken word.

Generalization: A rule or principle that is applicable in
               most reading situations.

SUMMARY

This chapter presented information on some of the terms and
the concepts they label as used by linguists and reading
teachers. Explanations and practice exercises on counting phonemes and on identification of voiced and unvoiced speech sounds
were included. Word identification clues were explained along
with syllabication and surface and deep structure of language.

Individual words are difficult to identify in speech. Words,
like phonemes, are not descrete units of speech except by pyscho-
logical categorization. Printed words define spoken words with
boundaries of space as confirmed by the dictionary and convention
or tradition. Although children need to learn to match words with
their spoken equivalents, meaning is signalled in context; not by
individual words. Meaning must be emphasized from the very beginning of reading instruction. While beginners need to identify
all of the words, skillful readers use a variety of word identification skills in context; configuration, or shapes of words,
picture clues, semantic, syntactic and structural or morphemic
clues.

Semantic clues help the reader to know that the context makes
sense while syntactic or grammatical clues are what make the
context sound right. Context clues help test the reader's
attempts to identify words by phonic analysis. Context clues are
also a basic means of word identification because they can direct
predictions or anticipated meanings.

Although, not strictly a word identification technique, skipping unrecognized words can be an efficient reading strategy when
the unrecognized word would not provide information to help the
reader understand. Looking for little words in big words is not
recommended as a word identification technique because it can be
misleading. To find fat and her in father would not be useful.

Finally, a Glossary of Phonic and Linguistic Terms was included at the end of this chapter. It contains terminology that
every teacher should know thoroughly.

References

Carroll, J.B. (1960). Language development, Encyclopedia of Educational Research. New York: Macmillan.

Durrell, D. (1971). An address given at the International Reading Association Rocky Mountain Regional Conference. Billings, Montana. Spring, 1971.

Elkonin, D.B. (1973). USSR. In J. Downing, ed. Comparative reading: Cross-national studies of behavior and processes in reading and writing. New York: Macmillan.

STUDY GUIDE QUESTIONS

1. Compare the job descriptions, or functions, of linguists or psycholinguists to those of reading teachers.

2. How might a knowledge of linguistics be helpful to a reading teacher?

3. What is the difference between phonemes and syllables?

4. What is the difference between phoneme perception and auditory discrimination?

5. What is the difference between surface structure and deep structure of language?

6. Which word identification clue answers the question :
   1). "Does it sound right?" and 2) "Does it make sense?"

7. Does a morpheme always represent meaning?

8. State the open-closed syllable rule.

9. Describe two ways to count syllables.

10. What is the main value of phonic knowledge for the identification of words.

CHAPTER IV

Teaching Strategies

Analytic and Synthetic Phonics

Just as the terms imply, analytic phonics analyzes whole words; synthetic phonics synthesizes speech sounds into whole words. Analytic phonics is not taking words apart, but looking at parts, focusing on likenesses and differences.

Auditory Blending

In the application of synthetic phonics, children practice auditory blending of phonemes (usually distorted) into whole words. Synthetic phonics is usually a deductive learning activity. Children are given phonic generalizations which are then applied to words. For instance children might be taught that the letter "b" says "buh" and "d" says "duh" or makes the "duh" sound. Children would be taught to identify and to produce short and long vowels. They would be told that when a vowel letter comes between two consonant letters it is usually short. So we'd blend "buh"-a-"duh" together to get "bad". Three phonemes would be synthesized into a whole word.

The teacher might even write "b" on the board and ask a pupil, "What sound does this letter make?" Most children are wise enough not to put their ear to the board to listen for the sound. Linguists are more concerned about scientific accuracy than with teaching children to read. Teachers are concerned with helping children learn to read and if they feel that it will be helpful to a child to tell them that letters talk or make sounds, then that is what they will do. It is somewhat traditional in teaching reading to tell children that letters talk and sometimes even to personify letters just as cartoonists have animals talk. Besides, it doesn't take children any longer to understand what the teacher means by letters making sounds than it does to understand what the science teacher means by sunrise and sunset.

Linguists have pointed out, to reading teachers, that a consonant phoneme cannot be pronounced in isolation from a vowel so that attempts to do so will produce distorted sounds. While this is true, it may not discredit the value of auditory blending since children are capable of guessing the correct pronunciation of words that have been synthesized from distorted phonemes. Groff (1986) found that "100% of the second graders tested could infer and produce the "o" of from as /u/ after first hearing it as /o/ " p.921.

Linguists generally feel that children can handle the truth about letter-sound relationships and can learn much easier when taught that speech is primary to print. In other words, speech is not determined by spelling. Speech can be produced even without a written language. Anthropologists speculate that cave people might have produced speech sounds even before there was any writing on the walls. Seriously though, there are still cultures that have no written language, yet they speak to each other. One of the roles of Christian missionaries in Africa has been to live among the people of an African tribe long enough to learn their language; then to assign graphemes to those speech sounds that are significantly different. When they have developed a writing system, the Holy Bible can then be written in that tribe's own language for them to read independently.

Analytic phonics would probably be preferred over synthetic phonics by most linguists. Speech sounds are represented by letters in the analytic phonics approach. Children would not be told that letters talk but that they represent, spell, or signal speech sounds. Just as kindergarten children learn terminology such as "lower-case" letters, beginning readers are capable of learning accurate terminology such as graphemes and phonemes. It may be easier for the beginner to have a new term such as "phoneme" to label a new concept than it would be to try to talk around it. Most basal reader textbooks emphasize an analytic phonics approach although auditory blending is taught as a worthwhile skill. Children would be helped to learn inductively that the vowel is usually short when surrounded by consonants. The teacher would put several words on the chalkboard as examples. The word "bad" could be learned by analogy. When the child knows Dad, sad, mad, and words that start like bad such as Bill, bat, ball, and big, then "bad" will just look more like /bad/ than like anything else.

Comparison of Analytic and Synthetic Phonics

Analytic	Synthetic
Preferred by linguists	Preferred by "phonic zealots"
Speech is primary to print	Print is primary
Induces generalizations	Generalizations deduced
Specific examples to rules	Rules first; then examples
Spelling patterns studied in word families	Uses auditory blending to combine phonemes
Emphasized in most basals	Used in "intensive" phonics

Alphabetic Clues to Mediation

Durrell (1980) reported that spelling was more than twice as effective for analyzing unknown words as was auditory blending for 240 primary grade children who had been taught "sounding" as the method of word attack. Durrell pointed out that the action of the speech mechanisms in spelling an unrecognized word is often similar to those used in pronouncing the word. Examples are such words as boil, post, spend, leap, frog, lemon, and smell. Any child who knows letter names can use the spelling method of word attack. This study confirms the observations of Donald Durrell and Helen Murphy in classrooms and clinics that led them to abandon, long ago, "sounding out" as a component of their phonic programs at Boston University.

Children frequently reply with the name of the letter, rather than the "sound" when the teacher coaches, "What sound does that word start with?"   And really, why should we teach children that "b" says "buh" when "buh" is no more accurate nor helpful than "bee"?   The classic First Grade Studies, reported by Bond and Dykstra (1967), concluded that letter-name knowledge of children entering first grade, as measured by the Murphy-Durrell Letter Names Test, was the best single predictor of reading achievement as measured by the Stanford Acheivement battery given at the end of first grade. Prediction is based upon correlation and correlation doesn't imply causation. Correlation between letter-name knowledge and reading acheivement is a strong positive relationship that also doesn't rule out causation. Research has failed to provide empirical evidence that children who are taught letter names will learn to read more efficiently but logic continues to recommend the early teaching of letter names. While kindergarten teachers do see children who can paint and draw letter shapes and name them without knowing their functions, Durrell (1980) has emphasized the value of letter-name knowledge for beginning readers. Only the names of h, q, w, and y have no relationship to the phonemes they represent. The other letters of the alphabet give a clue to the phoneme that they usually represent when we pronounce the name of the letter. For example:

1. The name of a vowel letter produces what teachers call the long vowel sound: /ae/, /ee/, /ie/, /oe/, and /ue/. Teachers who attribute vocal ability to letters sometimes tell their students that the "long vowel sound is the sound that you hear when the vowel says its own name.

2. The pronunciation of the following consonant letters produces the sound that the letter usually spells plus a long e sound ; i.e. /ee/:

    B, C, D, G, P, T, V, and Z.

3. The pronuciation of the following consonant letters produces the sound that the letter usually represents plus a long a sound; i.e. /ae/:

    J, K

4. The pronunciation of the following consonant letters produces the sound that the letter usually represents preceded by a short e sound; i.e. /eh/:

    F, L, M, N, X

5. The sound that the letter R usually spells can be heard in the pronunciation of the name of the letter.

So there is a case of logic involved in the letter-name controversy. Groff (1984) reviewed the literature on letter-name knowledge and concluded that, "Letter name teaching is appropriate if done concurrently with instruction in phonics" (p. 387). Another logical reason to teach letter names is for communication. It is easier to refer to letters by name than to have to say, "You know. The one that is shaped like a football goal post." Children who haven't learned to name letters can work on lower level tasks such as matching letters while the teacher names the letters that are matched.

Imagery Value of Words

What is the response to words when we are reading as a communication process, that is, reading for meaning? Is it really the pronuciation of words or thinking of the sounds of speech in silent reading? Well, if it is, that's just a preliminary step. It is the imagery that the words elicit that make it possible for the fluent reader to imagine a character, setting, or event described by the author's words. In fact, the author wrote words in an attempt to describe his or her own images. Response to printed words is not going from the surface structure of print to the surface structure of speech. Linguists tell us that we can't really do that and call it reading. The reader must get below the surface structure of language to the deep meaning, as closely as possible, to that intended by the author.

Hargis, C.H. & Gickling, E. E. (1978) compared the ease of sight word learning of high imagery words with low imagery words on kindergarten children and found that the high imagery words were learned more easily and remembered better than low imagery words.

Durrell (1980) pointed out that "Words are labels for remembered experiences; a spoken or printed word evokes the appropriate imagery-idea in the mind of the listener or reader" (p.161).

Phonemic Perception

Children really have no need to analyze and break up their language into segments such as sentences, words, syllables, or phonemes until they have to deal with writing; printed words. A child can speak and understand sentences, phrases, and words without any knowledge of where the separation would be in printed form. Even children who speak in complete sentences may write run-on sentences.

If we teach phonics to a child who has not learned to perceive and discriminate phonemes, that child may just learn which letters spell speech sounds that they do not hear within words. There is, therefore, little sense, to that child, in the way words are spelled since the letters are not associated with speech sounds that are perceived "within" words; even though that child can associate the letter with the sound in isolation. That child needs help; ear training in order to perceive and discriminate phonemes within spoken words. The following case will illustrate a typical example of a bright child's struggle to solve the mystery of how other children learned to read.

Durrell and Murphy (1953) described the case of a ten-year-old boy with a mental age of seventeen, an "enviable clarity and fluency of speech," and excellent phonics ability who had a reading vocabulary of only 60 words. He couldn't read! His intellect, his language facility, and his phonic knowledge only served to tell him which letters and combinations of letters were used to spell speech sounds. Nothing he had learned in five years of school had taught him how to read, despite his conscientiousness, because he had not yet discovered the "secret" prerequisite for learning to analyze and identify printed words.

After a diagnosis at the Boston University Reading Clinic revealed his lack of phoneme perception, he was given tutorial auditory training until he revealed, "I knew that there was a trick to it! The words have sounds in them and you just match the sound with the way the word looks. I suppose that's why they taught me phonics all these years." That boy subsequently gained eight years progress in reading acheivement in the next three months. This boy's predicament exemplifies the confusion that many children have in trying to relate reading instructional activities to the reading process.

Phonics training is just a discouraging ritual that has no application to reading for those frustrated learners who have not yet discovered the "secret" that spoken words have separate sounds within them. There are separate sounds within spoken words! These phonemes may be only psychological subdivisions or segmentations but learning to perceive or process them into categories is an essential prerequisite to learning to read. Such knowledge seems obvious to the literate adult who is tempted to assume that children must hear these sounds just because they are there. But there are enough children entering school each year, without this concept, to make a nucleus for a low group in each first-grade classroom.

The knowledge that spoken words can be further segmented into phonemic units does not descend upon children from their use of language. They are not likely to discover, from their own efforts, the "trick" to building a reading vocabulary. Those children who have not discovered the secret are likely to just become older illiterates until someone reveals to them that there are separate sounds within words. After they have learned to identify 60 to 75 written words, additional words are confused with those that are known. Without the ability to perceive and discriminate phonemes, the literacy learner is unable to process visual information, from printed words, into significant categories. The frustrated learner is unable to perceive the unique appearance of each word as being different from every other word. Such a reading disabled child cannot discern the distinctive features of each word.

Once the learner discovers that spoken words are composed of separate sounds, however, he or she is able to build a perceptual net of distinctive features as explained on pages 15 - 17, This perceptual net can then be used to catch and hold written words in a sight vocabulary as phonic and structural analysis skills accumulate. We must be careful not to let our adult view of reading, from our advanced cognitive development, influence how we think about how children might perceive words. It is tempting to believe that children must hear the sounds within words or they wouldn't be able to speak so clearly. That is an adult analysis of a child's problem. The reading process is so complex that is probably more amazing that so many of us are literate than it is that so many fail to learn to read.

Combine Pleasure with Word Drill

It is important to make our learning activities for word identification as pleasant as possible in order for the learner to approach reading with a positive attitude. There is very little enjoyment in drill on words so it is helpful for the teacher to present skill drills in a game format. It could be a word-card game of some kind, or a computer game.

Word identification tutorial and drill software for Computer Assisted Instruction (CAI) continues to accumulate and improve. Children still aren't tired of playing with the microcomputer. It puts them in control and does not judge them.

Of course, the most satisfactory rewards from word identification activities will result from the information obtained from actual reading; from comprehension. When a child enjoys the experience of living vicariously through the senses of a story character, the reading is relevant to desires. A child may receive aesthetic enjoyment from the mental pictures ellicited from the reading of a poem. Another rewarding type of information, obtainable from reading, explains how to do or construct something.

SUMMARY

This chapter on word identification teaching strategies is not intended to present methods for teaching word identification. A description and comparison of analytic and synthetic phonics was presented. Analytic phonics seems to be the most linguistically acceptable although the auditory blending of synthetic phonics can be a useful skill for mediating the identification of words.

Ability to name the letters of the Roman alphabet facilitates communication and provides useful clues to mediated word identification. It is recommended that beginners learn to identify and name the letters of the alphabet. Word identification is not complete until the surface structure of words evokes the imagery intended by the author. Word identification leads to the rich vivid imagery that facilitates comprehension. From her work with untrained people, a Professor of Art at California State University, Betty Edwards (1986), believes that anyone of sound mind can learn to draw. She suggests the possibility that the same is true for learning to read. She suggests that "... we are only now beginning to understand the complex dual functions, verbal and visual, of the human brain, and new possibilities are opening up" (p. 8).

Phoneme perception was suggested as a prerequisite to the ability to use phonics in mediating the identification of words. Ability to perceive and discriminate the significant sounds of speech makes orthography rational. It makes sense that words are spelled the way they are when the learner hears the sounds that the letters represent. To teach phonics to a child without the ability to perceive phonemes is to teach the child which letters spell sounds that the child does not hear within words. In these cases, children can learn 60 to 75 words before they all begin to look alike; the words, not the children.

Because there is a paucity of intrinsic pleasure in drill on word identification skills, it is recommended that fun games be employed. Learning centers equipped with microcomputers and word identification courseware can add variety and interest to otherwise dull drill and practice programs for word identification.

Teachers are cautioned not to fall into the temptation of attributing higher level cognitive development to children than is realistic.

References

Bond, G.L., & Dykstra, R. (1967). The cooperative research program in first-grade reading instruction. Reading Research Quarterly,7, 16-110.

Durrell, D. (1980). COMMENTARY: Letter-name values in reading and spelling, Reading Research Quarterly, 16 , 159.

_____. (1980). COMMENTARY: Semantic word recognition, Reading Research Quarterly, 16, 161.

Edwards, B. (1986). Drawing on the artist within. New York: Simon & Schuster.

Groff, P. (1984). Resolving the letter name controversey. The Reading Teacher, 37, 384-388.

_____ . (1986). The maturing of phonic instruction. The Reading Teacher, 39, 919-923.

Hargis, C.H. & Gickling, E.E. (1978). The function of imagery in word recognition development. The Reading Teacher,31,870 - 873.

STUDY GUIDE QUESTIONS

1. Is auditory blending emphasized in synthetic or analytic phonics? Which one?

2. Why do you feel that it does or does not serve a worthwhile purpose to tell children that letters talk, make sounds, or have sounds?

3. Describe two values of letter name knowledge for beginning readers.

4. What is the best single predictor, in September of first grade, of June reading acheivement?

5. What might be the role or value of imagery for word identification?

6. What might be a reason that a fourth grader cannot build a sight vocabulary even with a high IQ and a thorough command of phonics, other than **dyslexia**?

7. Describe one activity that might make word identification skills learning pleasant and enjoyable.

8. Name and describe two CAI software programs for tutoring or drill & practice on word identification. Give complete reference and ordering information.

9. What does phoneme perception mean and why is it important?

10. What evidence is there that second grade children could mediate the correct pronunciation of the word **"from"** from the separate distorted sounds /fer/- /uh/- /m/?

———

Here is an opportunity for you to test yourself on your knowledge
of word identification concepts and content. See how well you
can do. The answers are given at the end of the quiz so that you
can correct your own paper. If you don't get at least 70%, you
need to review those items that you missed.

WORD IDENTIFICATION QUIZ

MULTIPLE CHOICE: Draw a line around the letter before the one
best or correct answer for each of the items below. After
you've indicated your choices, check them with the answers on
the page following the quiz. GOOD LUCK!!!!

1. The most linguistically accurate definition of a vowel is:

    A.   the letters a,e,i,o,u and sometimes y and w
    B.   a speech sound restricted by much audible friction
    C.   an open speech sound produced with a minimum of friction
    D.   a sound in the middle of a word

2. The most frequent spelling pattern in primary grade words is:

    A.   CVC B.   VCE C.   CIVIC   D.   CVVC

3. A reader who applies the understanding that the letter "c"
   stands for the "soft" sound when followed by e, i, or y, is
   making use of a _____ clue.

    A.   phonic B.   linguistic   C.   semantic   D.   syntactic

4. A morpheme is:

    A.   the smallest meaningful unit of language
    B.   a representation of a basic sound unit
    C.   the final sound in a syllable
    D.   the smallest class of significant speech sounds

5. Most basal readers:

   A.   base the first grade program primarily on auditory blending.
   B.   provide very little help with phonics
   C.   use the synthetic approach to phonics instruction
   D.   use the analytic approach to phonics instruction.

6. Context clues, structural analysis, dictionary aids, sight words, and phonics are classified as _____ skills.

   A.   basal reader   B.   word identification
   C.   dictionary   C.   oral reading

7. Intelligent guessing is often _____ for mediated word identification.

   A.   a desireable procedure   B.   of no value
   C.   pure luck   D.   inefficient

8. Context clues deal with:

   A.   usefulness   B.   meaning
   C.   picture clues   D.   surface structure of language

9. Which of the following techniques is NOT recommended as a strategy for mediated word identification?

   A.   looking for little words within the bigger word
   B.   circling the prefix and/or suffix
   C.   identifying the syllables in a word
   D.   analysis of syllables for orthographic patterns

10. Which of the following statements is NOT true?

   A.   phonic knowledge is helpful for fluent reading.
   B.   ear training should precede sight training.
   C.   Phoneme perception is prerequisite to phonics application.
   D.   English is so irregular that phonics is of little value.

11. The letter "i" represents the _____ in the word "pencil".

   A.   sound signalled by the "i" in "prince". B.   schwa sound
   C.   short sound of "i"   D.   the short sound of "u"

12. The "br" signals a _____ in the word "brown".

   A.   consonant digraph   B.   consonant blend
   C.   phoneme   D.   diphthong

13. How many consonant digraphs are there in the word diphthong?

   A.   None B.   1   C.   2   D.   3

14. How many diphthongs are there in the word digraph?

   A.   None B.   1   C.   2   D.   3

15. In which of the following words does "oo" signal the long sound?

   A.   took B.   broom   C.   brook   D.   stood

16. If "eb" were a syllable in a word, the letter "e" in that syllable would probably represent the same phoneme as does the "e" in the word:

   A.   ending   B.   peach   C.   feet D.   me

17. If "pu" were a syllable in a word, the letter "u" in that syllable would probably represent the same phoneme as does the "u" in the word:

   A.   umbrella B.   punish   C.   auditory D.   united

18. The letter "a" in the word "along" stands for the:

   A.   short sound of "u" B.   short sound of "a"
   C.   sound signalled by the letter "a" in 1water2.
   D.   schwa sound

19. How many syllables are there in the word **parasitic?**

    A.   2   B.   3   C.   4   D.   5

20. How many phonemes are there in the word **oxen?**

    A.   3   B.   4   C.   5   D.   6

21. How many phonemes are there in the word **parallel?**

    A.   4   B.   5   C.   6   D.   7

22. English contains about _____ phonemes?

    A.   26   B.   30   C.   44   D.   62

23. Which of the words below does <u>NOT</u> contain a diphthong?

    A.   oil   B.   know   C.   toy   D.   how

24. In which of the words below does "th" signal the voiced sound?

    A.   them   B.   diphthong   C.   ether   D.   breath

25. Identify the one word below that does <u>NOT</u> contain a consonant digraph according to the traditional definition for reading.

    A.   sing   B.   comb   C.   tough   D.   machine

26. If krasp were a real word, the letter "a" would likely stand for the sound represented by the letter "a" in the word:

    A.   matter   B.   acorn   C.   cart   D.   adore

27. If snup were a real word, the letter "u" would likely stand for the sound spelled by the letter "u" in:

    A.   super   B.   stupid   C.   cube   D.   supper

28. If gep were a real word, the letter "g" would likely
    represent (according to the rule) the same phoneme as the "g"
    in:

    A.   gate   B.   gypsy   C.   gulp   D.   agate

29. If bax were a real word, the letter "a" would likely
    represent the same phoneme as does the "a" in:

    A.   water   B.   answer   C.   adore   D.   acorn

Identify the one word in each item that begins with a schwa
sound.

30. A.   average   B.   angel   C.   author   D.   arrive

31. A.   udder   B.   using   C.   upon D.   understand

32. A.   ostrich   B.   approach C.   attic   D.   emblem

In each of the items listed below, identify the one word that
begins with a short vowel sound:

33. A.   ideal   B.   income   C.   irk D.   ice

34. A.   endless   B.   early   C.   easy D.   ecology

35. A.   action   B.   angel   C.   author   D.   arrive

In each of the items listed below, identify the one word that
begins with a long vowel sound:

36. A.   emblem   B.   early   C.   edge   D.   easy

37. A.   able   B.   ask   C.   apple   D.   about

38. A.   improvise B.   ice   C.   instant   D.   irrigate

TRUE-FALSE:

For the items below, Mark T before the number of the item if you
think that it is TRUE and F if you believe it is FALSE:

39. Vowels are always voiced.

40. The fewer the number of clues needed to identify the word, the quicker the identification.

41. The word high is a closed syllable. (Be careful)

42. Vowel letters followed by the consonant /r/ usually represent the short vowel sound.

43. Phonic analysis is the most efficient method of word identification.

44. The study of significant speech sounds of a particular language is known as:

A. phonics   B. phonetics
C. phonemics   D. linguistics

45. Which of the following is **NOT** one of the steps in skill development identified by Fitz & Posner?

A. Cognitive   B. Affective
C. Conditioning   D. Automaticity

46. Words are most efficiently put into a child's sight vocabulary from repeated:

A. tachistoscopic exposure at 1/100 of a second.
B. response in meaningful content.
C. exposure of flash cards with feedback.
D. tracing over textured surfaces.

47. Cues for word identification that are found in context and that have to do with the meaning of known words are called:

A. semantic B. syntactic C. spelling D. orthographic

48. The order or arrangement of words and the way they relate to one another is referred to as:

A. syntax   B. sequence   C. structure D. semantics

49. Significant speech sounds within words of a particular language are called:

A. phonic units   B. graphemes   C. letters   D. phonemes

50. In phonics, the <u>schwa</u> refers to:

A.   a vowel blend   B.   a diphthong
C.   a vowel digraph   D.   an unaccented vowel

* * * * * * * * *

Answers to the Word Identification Quiz

1. C	13. D	25. B	37. A	49. D
2. A	14. A	26. A	38. B	50. D
3. A	15. B	27. D	39. T	
4. A	16. A	28. B	40. T	
5. D	17. D	29. B	41. F	
6. B	18. D	30. D	42. F	
7. A	19. C	31. C	43. F	
8. B	20. C	32. B	44. C	
9. A	21. D	33. B	45. B	
10. D	22. C	34. A	46. B	
11. B	23. B	35. A	47. A	
12. B	24. A	36. D	48. A	

INDEX